What A
Mother Says

List of books published by Juanita Pittman-Brown:

Words in Bloom   published 2005

What A Mother Says

A Collection of Affirmations, Quotes and Art

Juanita Pittman-Brown

iUniverse, Inc.
New York Lincoln Shanghai

What A Mother Says
A Collection of Affirmations, Quotes and Art

iUniverse books may be ordered through booksellers or by contacting:

iUniverse
2021 Pine Lake Road, Suite 100
Lincoln, NE 68512
www.iuniverse.com
1-800-Authors (1-800-288-4677)

Because of the dynamic nature of the Internet, any Web addresses or links contained in this book may have changed since publication and may no longer be valid.

Illustrations by: Dillon Addis of Abbeville, South Carolina.

ISBN: 978-0-595-45774-8 (pbk)
ISBN: 978-0-595-90076-3 (ebk)

Printed in the United States of America

This book is dedicated to Kevin Dean Brown, son of Juanita Pittman-Brown, for his encouragement and inspiration to write this book and to Katrine Pitts, her high-school typing teacher, who had a profound influence on Juanita's education. Too, Juanita fondly remembers Nettie Young, her eighth grade English teacher, and Frances Sheely, her high-school English teacher for their compassion, instruction, and kindness in her formative years.

INTRODUCTION

This book is a collection of Juanita Pittman-Brown's aphorisms. Juanita's son, Kevin, suggested that his mother compile the quotes which she had so freely shared and written over the years into a book. He said that he believed others would enjoy the wisdom of her words. Juanita shares in this book her aphorisms as a masterpiece collection.

CONTENTS

ANGELS

* Mothers are angels set free.

* An angel is protection in its truest form.

* Angels bear the burdens of those who have no wings.

* Angels show you the way when the veil of life shades your view.

* When you pray for direction, keep in mind that angels are often the ones who show you the way.

* If you look for angel wings, you may see angels.

* An angel leaves a feather as a token of God's grace.

BEAUTY

* Beauty on the other side of the mountain awaits you after you have crossed the hurdle before you.

* To see beauty you must look through eyes that see past the darkness sometimes in the world; for the light will only shine in the sky of your life when you wait for the clouds to pass.

* Beauty in the moment becomes tomorrow's dream.

* The greater the refinement of a gem, the more beautiful the sparkle.

* There is empowerment in silently seeking and visualizing the beauty and expectation of tomorrow.

* Laughter paints a day a beautiful color of joy.

* Life's beauty presents itself as a reality today and a memory tomorrow.

* Beauty is free to the eye of the pure soul.

* Travels of the soul have a final destination and make for a more beautiful journey.

* Bad makes good look beautiful.

* Beauty of life may become your reality today and your memory tomorrow.

* Aging and life truly are beautiful when viewed with eyes of the soul.

* In the sunlight of the soul, the beauty of a child can be viewed as a priceless treasure.

* Colors of butterflies and flowers paint life as beautiful as it truly is.

*   While a rose may prick your finger,
    its fragrance will dazzle your nose.

BLESSING

* The offering of a child is the blessing of a day.

* Double offering brings double blessing.

* What we give is often the over-abundance of that we have received and what we receive often is what we gave in our own need.

* It takes effort to be a blessing; it takes an open heart to receive a blessing; it takes open hands to share a blessing.

* If dreams were pennies and blessings were dollars, I would consider myself wealthy beyond measure.

* The difference between luck and blessing is a holy equation.

* An offering is a down-payment on a blessing.

* Counting our blessings teaches us how to multiply our dreams.

* With forgetting comes forgiving and the blessing of acceptance.

* Blessings abide where children spread their smiles, joy, and purity.

* A grain of sand of kindness returns to you in an ocean of blessings.

CHARACTER TRAITS

* Giving your best is the perfect way to become what you are intended to be.

* What is in the heart sings the loudest song.

* No is no because yes holds options that would destroy.

* It is not what I am or what I have by which I can be defined; it is what I have to offer.

* Trust is like an egg; it is fragile, and if the shell is broken, the goodness spills out.

* Trust is necessary when treasure is shared.

* Give your children diamonds and granite, and they will be balanced and not cling to either.

* Rudeness digs a deep ditch.

* Anger and frustration sometimes create the impetus for change.

* Not commenting sometimes is the best answer of all.

* It is in disorder that we find there is reason for change and order finds its place.

* When you find your way, make sure you keep the map.

* A moment spent in doing well is never wasted.

* If you have a thought which is not good or pure, it is best to have a second thought.

* A father finds a way when there is no way.

* A father is a drink of cool water on a hot day.

* Excuses are the result of poor judgment.

* Bad is not becoming.

* A father is the ocean beneath the ship of a life.

* The way of the heart weaves along a winding road.

* A greedy heart begins with an unfulfilled desire.

* Effort may be necessary for a positive outcome.

* Acceptance may be a requirement, and peace may be the prize.

* Timing may be the fire beneath the pot.

* Old age may be the greener pasture of your soul.

* Money is not enough to clean a dirty spirit.

* A father is the oar on a boat.

* If you wish to consume your energy, why not use it where there is the most need or the greatest joy.

* Stillness in the night allows the soul to hear and the mind to comprehend.

* Character shines forth when there is difficulty or loss.

* What you hang on the clothes-line of your life will be refreshed by the sunshine of others.

* Labor by the hands of the pure soul never ends.

* It is through open-ness and trust that children discover what the world has to offer.

* Children are open and trusting, and it is in this combination that they discover what the world has to offer.

* Let no man answer for you; let no man accept your consequence; for no other man can accept or handle what you are due.

* It is through our generosity that necessity finds a friend.

* The garden of the soul is the place the most precious fruit is cultivated and grown.

* Sometimes it is better to be alone; if not to be alone puts you in bad company.

* Every minute you spend in negativity is a minute you do not spend in the positive.

* When difficult times are present, be sure fear is absent.

* To be eccentric only means you are the opposite of dull.

* A willing heart is a fertile field for the heavenly sower.

* A good result began with a positive thought.

* Never forget that to be of value first you must know your own worth.

* Divinity finds its way into the hearts of those who seek its presence.

* The mother of persecution has no peace in old age.

* A minute holds the same opportunity for all.

* How you respond reveals the true self.

* Those who humiliate become the humiliated.

* Go with the flow; you never know in which pond you will row your boat.

* Justice is metered by honesty.

* If you hang out with those who seek the lesser of good, you will find that bad will become your friend.

* If you keep your conscience clean, you will not wear a dress of deceit.

* Your worth was determined before your birth.

* What you place in the drawer of your heart may greet you with the sun of day.

* Sometimes the prodigal years are the very reason redemption is ever realized.

* To be narrow limits your view.

* Skill is not enough to paint a hardened heart soft.

* Spread joy about your day for it may be the sunshine of tomorrow.

* Too late is never trying.

* To help someone else makes you the brightest star in the sky.

* Measure not your worth by the scales of human eyes.

* It is not imperative that your reality be my reality.

* Pleasure is not promised, but strength to persevere is.

* A watch without hands is like man without good works.

* Laughter is the song of the heart.

* It is in our humility that we find our reality.

* The sturdiness of the spirit grows from the grounded roots of the Irish tree.

* Those anointed are those appointed.

* The helping hand of the kind soul is often the redeeming source for the soul in need.

* Courage is perseverance in action.

* The car, the house, the clothes do not the man make.

COMPASSION

*   It is through our compassion that we find who we truly are; it is through the needs of others that we discover the true meaning of compassion; it is through compassion and need that we discover the mercy of God.

*   Compassion can be shown but cannot be bought.

*   Skill can be paid for, but no dollar value can be placed on compassion.

*   God is the foundation of mercy and compassion.

*   Compassion is born in the heart and expressed through family and friends.

DREAMS

* Hospitality is a warm bed, soft covers, and a dream heaven-sent.

* Little pleasures keep big dreams alive.

* Dream dreams that are bigger than you are; for God is the one who gave you your dream.

* If you dream of greater things, greater things will come to you.

* When the dreams you have do not match God's plan, it is best to go back to sleep and dream again.

* When dreams are the colors of your night, you may create the painting of the day.

* The painting of your dream sometimes is painted with the brush of God, and the colors are the people He places in your life.

* The sun shines; days pass; fun is had; and dreams do come true.

* Dreams are the future thoughts of innocent souls.

* Dreams are the colors used by God to paint our lives.

* Dreams transcend our daily lives and take us to places that free our minds, inspire our souls, and lead us to a fuller understanding.

* Your dream in the night may become the reality of your day.

* Little boys, big dreams, and small talk make each day new.

* With each breath we share the richness of the day and hopeful dreams in the night.

* God instills a desire in a heart; faith fuels the flame; and a dream is born.

* If no one believes in your dream but God, that is enough.

* Imagination has no boundaries as dreams have no limits.

*   Every child is blessed with innocence and the dream of life yet to be.

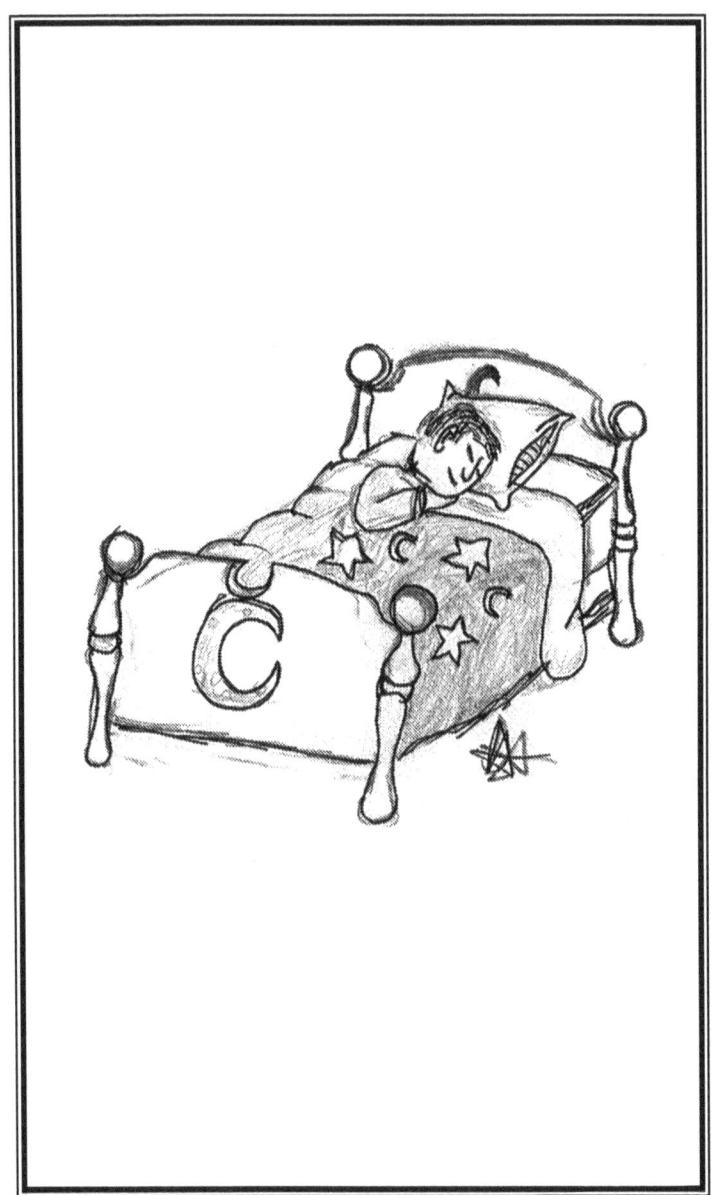

FAITH

* Faith is the sun in your day that lights the way.

* When you look for the way, be sure that you hold the hand of faith.

* If faith is in your plan, you are on your way to success.

* Faith, vision, and joy share a common bond.

* The mustard seed of today may become the flourishing plant of your life tomorrow.

* Faith reminds us that through our belief we arrive.

* Faith is being out on the limb of the tree owned by God.

* Know that faith is a seed that you plant in the garden of your heart; from this seed grows the fruit of a life.

* If you can tell me how to forgive, I can tell you how to know true joy.

FORGIVENESS

* When you love someone, forgiveness is easy.

* Forgiveness has no memory and tells tomorrow that all things are new.

* Forgiveness is easy when love is present.

* Would you forgive if you wish to be forgiven?

* What forgiveness gives you is far more than you being unforgiving could ever offer.

* Forgiveness is fuel for the soul.

* Over the hill of forgiveness is the sea of forgetfulness.

FRIENDSHIP

*   Harmony is expressed in the tapestry of friendship.

*   Friendship is a treasured jewel of two souls.

*   A true friend will be there when they have nothing to gain.

*   Friendship is like an old barn; it survives the elements and remains as a shelter from the storms of life.

*   Friends are the warm covers of your heart.

*   Open minds, willing hearts, and kind words are often the beginning of friendship.

* A warm breeze, a sunny day, a walk with a friend; what more of life could I ask?

* Friends are jewels you meet along your path.

* Love conquers what unkindness creates.

* Friendship is refreshed by the showers of life and blooms as the flowers of well-spent time.

* A friend is the one who allows you to share your own space with yourself.

* To be friends means that you walked in the same pasture and managed to clean each others shoes.

HOPE

* When hope is your companion, the way is made less difficult.

* What we hope for may be the reason hope exists.

* The memories of struggle may be gone when hope of tomorrow comes.

* Joy finds a way to shine even when hope hides behind the cloudy sky of life.

* If you could tell me what hope means, then I would know that you have followed a path of faith, effort, and perseverance.

* Hope may be the sunshine in your day after the struggle of your night.

* Would hope be your vision of tomorrow when you see before you a mountain of difficulty today?

* Hope rises when the need is there; and victory arrives when there is no other way.

* Hope yields the way when you cannot see past your darkest hour.

* Hope reveals the best within and creates greatness to be.

KINDNESS

* Being ugly or unkind has no color, no age, and no style.

* When you measure your share of kindness, remember God was the provider of your portion.

* Love is the offering of a cool drink by a kind hand.

* Rain is to the earth as kindness is to love.

* Never be unkind; it is not necessary or becoming.

* There is always time to be kind.

* Being kind is like having a savings account which when needed pays more than expected.

* Being an adult is not a license for rudeness, but it is a requirement for kindness.

* Kindness is like a cool drink on a hot summer's day.

* A glass of lemonade and warm words bring sunshine to a day.

* Food for the soul is prepared by the hand of kindness and the heart filled with love.

* Returning love for unkindness takes the poison out of the sting.

* A kind manner is the only one to have in an unkind matter.

* Sparing others feelings is important because one day the kindness you

showed will be the very thing you need when you need it the most.

* Kindness and generosity are by far two of the greatest gifts.

* Kindness not received well will return to its owner.

* Kindness reaches forth just as unkindness keeps a closed pose.

LESSONS

* How you treat others is an expression of the way you were treated and the lessons you have learned.

* What we live, we learn; what we learn, we live; what we live and learn, we become.

* Training is training because it remains when thinking disappears.

* Division is unnecessary because it weakens the equation.

* Learning where necessity ends reveals where generosity begins.

* Learning occurs when eyes have seen, ears have heard, and hearts have been touched.

* Doing right is the best way to correct wrong.

* Lessons are learned from mess-ups to clean-ups as children become grown-ups.

* The shepherd corrects His flock for the good of all.

* The lessons of life if passed give you credentials for the life to come.

* Lessons come from fun, and fun comes with boys.

*   Instructions are only a guide to keeping you on target.

LIFE

*   Giving your best may be the offering that is required.

*   Live today; plan tomorrow; worry never.

*   A life without a mission is like a carpenter without his tools.

*   Never regret the past; it is preparation for the tomorrows of your life.

*   A car without wheels is like a life without God.

*   If when life is over, be sure that you realize that temporal and spiritual money are of different currencies.

* Be assured that destiny will have its own design in your life.

* At the toll bridge of life, there is no charge at the entrance; but the exit fee is always the same.

* Simple pleasures are the luxuries of life.

* When life is knocking at your door, be sure you are at home.

* It is best to keep our life simple, for it is difficult at best.

* Life is a gift, and what you do with it is a choice.

* If time is a treasure, then the treasure-chest is a life.

* Children, smiles, and hope are the substance of the true significance of life.

* When wisdom is shared, compassion and respect are the lessons learned.

* The greatest gift a child can give his parents is to live well.

* Watch your step for the next step is the beginning of the journey of a lifetime.

* Days are pennies; memories are dollars; and tomorrows are interest gained.

* The harvest of life is the product of the heavenly sower.

* The tributaries of a life hold the sweetest surprises.

* Life holds for every participant an opportunity for greatness of spirit.

* When the storms of life come, be sure that your sails have all been repaired and are intact.

* Time is a measure of this life that ends when eternity begins.

* Memories are the type-set of a life.

* A life not lived fully is a life where negativity stole a portion of one's day.

* Know that the sun on the horizon holds for you the promise of a day.

* Swinging in the sunshine is one way to view freedom first-hand.

* If we thank God for the sunshine and joy in our lives, we must also thank Him for the rain and tears in our lives.

* Forever is the answer when never is the question.

* Yesterday was a gift; today is a reality; tomorrow is a plan.

* A cup of coffee, a soft breeze, and warm thoughts start the best of days.

* Life always offers opportunity for change.

* Life is a joy in the present; a hope of the future; and remembrance of the past.

* When life takes a toll on you, be sure you have tokens in hand.

* The life you lead will be determined by your value of time.

* Balancing the books of life is done by holy hands.

* The sharing of two souls is the reality of today and the sweet memory of tomorrow.

* If you consider opportunity your friend, you may find that you have a companion for life.

* The world becomes a better place when a grandmother teaches from the heart.

* You cannot live on yesterday's successes, but you can live on today's hope and tomorrow's dreams.

* Listen with kindness; look with wonder; hear with understanding; and watch with amazement.

* Celebration of life at times comes in the form of sharing moments in a given day.

* Life keeps no secrets, and death has no voice.

* Snowflakes, day-dreams, and puppy-dog tails all are the interesting mix of the stuff of life.

* Life is like a butterfly; it is both fragile and beautiful.

* The summer sun, the beach, sea shells, and gulls on wing teach a child the meaning of living in the moment.

* Frantic is not a way to live, but joyful is a way to die.

* A day is the canvas for the brush of your life.

* The narrow worn path of today is sometimes the reason the walk-way of tomorrow exist.

* Coming home is the best gift after a long journey; for home is the place where you can plan, dream, and aspire for greater things.

* The day before you will present to you the canvas for the paint of your life.

* Life is a detour to a final destination.

* Life will be no greater or no less than that for which you aspire.

* As the seasons turn, so does the wonder of life.

* A path forks; a man chooses; a life begins; and a destiny is realized.

* A storage building is for storing, and a life is for giving.

* Happy may be defined as spending time with your family and laughing at the simple antics of a cat.

* The end of life allows the painting of a masterpiece by the perfect artist.

* Living in the moment allows you not to miss the day at hand.

* Honey bees, lady bugs, and butterflies may paint the sky of your life with joy.

LOVE

*   Where discipline abides, love abounds; and respect is gained.

*   Listen to your parents; they were children before you.

*   A mother answers a question with love even when the answer is no.

*   Children bloom best in the garden of love.

*   To ask is to care, and to listen is to love.

*   Love embraces; truth reveals; and destiny speaks.

*   A heart filled with love reaches out through the hands of a child.

* What you cannot respect and admire is not worthy of your time and love.

* Love blooms best in the garden of the soul.

* Love is viewed best in the window of the heart.

* Love is the potion of the pure spirit.

* Love what you live; live what you love.

* Judge no one, fear no one, hate no one, and love all; judgment is not our business, fear is counter-productive, hate is the opposite of love, and love is always right.

* Comfort cannot be measured, but love may be endless.

* Love multiplies when shared.

* When you think of me, always think of you; because without you, there is no me.

* When you are far away, remember the moon you see is the moon viewed by me.

* Love may be the protector of the innocent soul.

* It is through love's hand that life's lessons are taught and values take root.

* Sharing is the sunlight of the day, and love is the warmth of the night.

* Time shared is love gained.

* A heart that is filled with love always shares its abundance with others.

MOTHERHOOD

* A mother listens when the world turns away.

* A mother lights the candle of a life.

* Memories will exist because of the NOW.

* Light is a shadow turned inside-out.

* What is shared by little boys in play is relived in the minds of men.

* Memories are the roses of the soul.

* To live fully, you first must find what empty really is.

* As you embark on the road of life, be sure that you have a trustworthy vehicle and you have gas in your tank.

* Remembering is a gift of the life lived and the people loved.

* Deciding sometimes is the toughest decision you will ever make.

* Have you ever invited your children to spend eternity with you in heavenly light?

* Time is fleeting; love is enduring; and forever began with your first breath.

* Would a little bird sing if it had no reason to give thanks?

* Children are the gold of the mining of a life.

* If you use up your have to's and your want to's, there will be very few can do's.

* Relative understanding creates a basis for a common ground.

* Better to be the silent one than to be the silenced one.

* Winning is easy when fun is the prize.

* Rich is not a permanent condition.

* A grand-daughter is the light of a thousand years.

* When you are looking for the best in others, you may discover the very best in yourself.

* A mother is an architect of a life.

* A mother is the one who holds out her hand and reaches back with love.

* Must you ponder that wrinkles may ever appear; for they will and do, and they are the expression of the travels of your soul?

* If I tell you what makes me happy, will you tell me what makes you sad?

* Courage is perseverance in the truest form.

* When you look into the face of a child, remember that this is where innocence smiles.

* Where one's treasure abides so does one's heart.

* The one who controls the bridle of life controls the way.

* To share yourself, first you must know who you are.

* Tilling of a life will prepare the ground for a mighty harvest of the soul.

* Life is God's test track for the highways of heaven.

* You do not have to have a tired body to have a hurt heart.

* Tamper not with the business of another because you may find that their problems will share ownership with you.

* Freedom is knowing fun is forever.

* A safe child is the greatest treasure; a happy child is the greatest joy.

* Destiny is realized through colorful dreams, sweet memories, and soulful melodies.

* Listen to others, and then decide if you should add their thoughts to your heart.

* Time is priceless; thoughts are endless; and excuses are a waste.

* Courtesy is a by-product of a Christ-like attitude.

* No rule results in no control.

* If you close the blinds of your life, you may be closing out the sunshine of others.

* A mother shares her sunshine even on a rainy day.

* A mother remembers when the world has forgotten.

* A mother is the blue of the sky when your universe seems gray.

* A mother is present when the world has walked away.

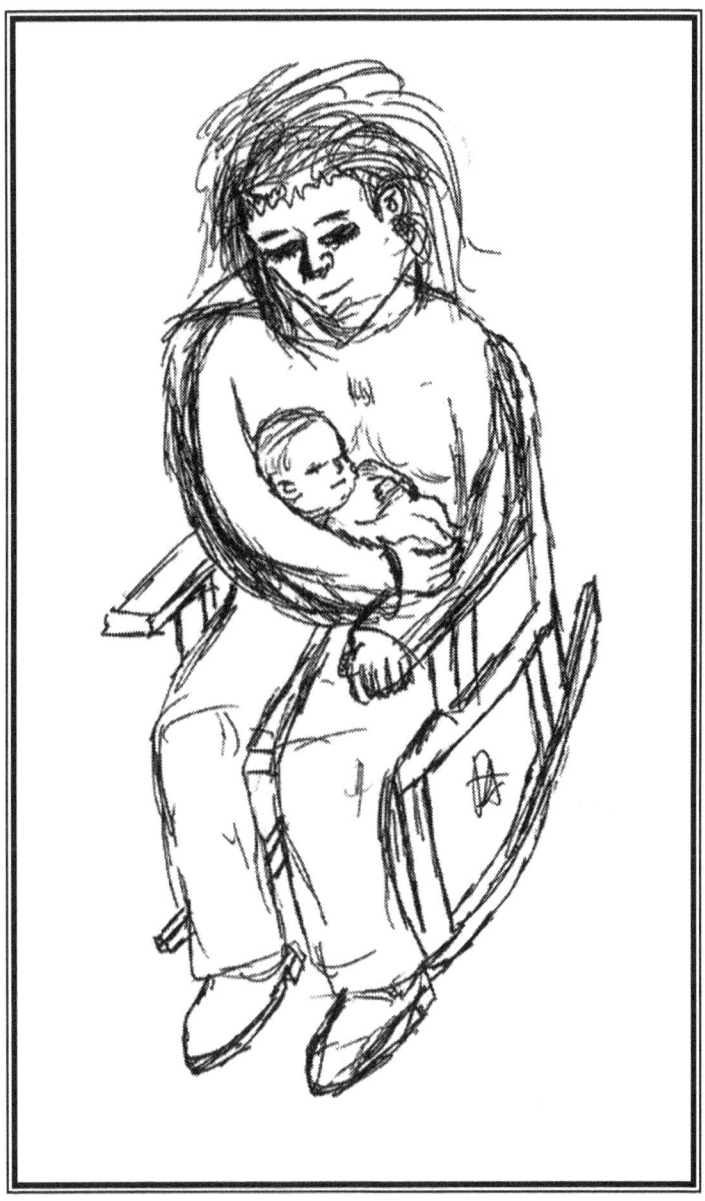

PRAYER

* Prayer is free, and God's answers are infinite and priceless.

* Problems make prayers productive.

* The time you spend in prayer is never truly lost.

* The only way to find the best that life has to offer is to remain prayerful, hopeful, and open to all possibilities.

* Through prayer we ask; through silence we hear; and through faith we see.

* Prosperity is the product of promise, praise, and prayer.

* The world's power is fueled by money; God's power is fueled by prayer.

* Prayer is the best option when success is the goal.

* Prayer is tattle-telling to God about a situation that has created discomfort for you as His child.

* Prayer is often the glue that connects God's people and provides connection to God.

RESPECT

*   What you respect shows you what you value.

*   If respect is given, remorse may be unnecessary.

*   A bad attitude has no respect for the company it keeps.

*   Respect is allowing for differences.

*   The way you treat others is the very means by which God will treat you.

*   Keeping a secret is ultimate respect.

*   Respect is answering in the positive when negative thoughts appear.

* If you respect others, you will find that you have more time to spend to make your life the best it can be.

SMILES

*   Smiles are often the greatest wealth we will ever know.

*   God does not smile when we misbehave.

*   For every tear cried, there is a smile waiting to be shared.

*   Where healing begins, smiles follow.

*   The winner in you makes the heart within me smile.

*   A smile is contagious, and its value is priceless.

*   You may never know the value of a smile you shared with one who had a need of which you were unaware.

* The offering of a smile is a potent remedy for sadness.

* Smiles tell where you have been and often tell you where you are going.

* Never doubt what a smile can mean to one who has none to give.

* If you smile at life, you will find that the view is better than if you view it with a frown.

* Smiles are carried by those who have full hearts and shared because their hearts over-flow.

* If you share a smile, you may find that when you need one that one will be shared freely with you.

* Happiness may reveal itself in the smile upon the face.

* If you are smiling, you may find that the world looks a little brighter and it welcomes you along your way.

* If a smile could be caught, what would you do with it if you caught it?

* The joy and the pleasure of being in a child's company will bring a smile in the most unexpected ways.

SPIRITUALITY

* A mule presents a stubborn streak to his master as man displays resistance to a loving God.

* What we live is who we are; what we become is who God designed.

* Where God abides, evil flees.

* Never forget that your example is the mold used by God to imprint the life of another.

* When testing comes, it is up to the student of life to be prepared for the exam of God.

* We struggle in our humanity, and we arrive in God's divinity.

* What you think you will never do will be the next thing on God's agenda for your life.

* Life is a patch-work quilt in that it is made up of the scraps pieced together by God's colorful designs.

* Healing of a life occurs when you turn to God who is the eternal physician.

* A lifetime of problems can be overcome with a moment spent with God.

* A star sparkles because God lights the heavens with love.

* Birth is our reminder that divine appointment is on the calendar of God.

* The canvas is life; the paint forms the design; and the artist is God.

* Don't think how … think God will.

* One day I will take my writings to God as my homework, and He will give me the grade I deserve with impartial grading.

* The accounting by God for the provision of a child is a tough audit.

* The sound of joy is God's soft whisper.

* Graduation is the next step toward independence in the world and dependence on God.

* You know you are successful when jealousy shows its face, and you know you have arrived when God fills your space.

* Worthy is the way of the one who follows God's precepts.

* Family is the connection, and God is the glue.

* God said HE WILL so that WE MAY.

* Stubbornness can be turned to faith only through contending as God ordains.

* God made provision for our redemption, and it is up to us to access His plan and keep our policy current.

* If you feel you are not on God's schedule, get another calendar.

* The greatest asset to the human spirit is one's relationship with God Almighty.

* The name is the mark placed by man; the soul is the mark placed by God.

* In order for you to be on time where God would have you arrive, sometimes you must be detained by mountains of issues and crooked roads of aggravation; but the end result will be a valley of peace, and the sun will rise tomorrow to make for a better day.

* Birth is God's renewal plan for mankind.

* If you have a spiritual journey to make, be sure that your vehicle is God-worthy.

* A vow is a direct promise before God, and you become accountable to God ultimately.

* When you look at the moon, remember the light you see shines only because God allows it.

* When you are defined by God, what your definition is will be written by His hand and the choices you make will be the words God writes.

* There is an accounting that we all must give, and that is to God; for He has final say.

* Anything ugly said or done must be explained to our parent God; I am only a sibling.

* Marriage is the jewel faceted by God; it is flawless in every way.

* The seed is the plan; the bud is the mold; and the blossom is the expression of the handiwork of God.

* A time to hate is never on the clock of God.

* God will not bring new furniture into a dirty house.

* God is like a candy store, but you do not pay with a charge card.

* If you seek credit from God, be sure you are able to pay the bill.

* The grace of God has no price tag.

* The finest moments known to man are the moments he spends in worshipping God.

* A sunset is the soft touch of God.

* When God gives you a trial, expect that He will use the result to its fullest extent.

* A lighted path began with the eternal spark of God.

* God owns the garden, but He gave me a hoe.

* When God keeps you from sleep in the night, it is because He has work to do; and you have not given Him time during the day.

* Error by man needs white-out by God.

* To bear your cross is to accept your humanity and God's divinity.

* The farther you run from God, the "behinder" you get.

* Standards are God's criteria for a journey to perfection.

* Providence is God's divinity protecting us from our own accidents.

SUCCESS

* Honor and success come to those who work hard, live well, and speak truth.

* Wisdom and learning lead to success when time is used wisely.

* A persistent spirit and willing hands are necessary for success.

* When others see your success, they only see your prosperity; they do not see the process.

* What you find at the end is the result of your beginning, perseverance, and determination to succeed.

* When someone says you can't, ask God how can I; when someone says you

won't, ask God will I; when someone says you will fail, ask God how you can succeed; when someone says you made it, tell them to give God thanks for you.

* It takes courage to endure, and it takes effort to succeed.

* To succeed, you first must know what you have to gain.

* Perseverance may be the necessary ingredient for success.

* Delivery is dependent on determination.

* If you think inside the box, you will stay inside the box.

* The potential reality of success, I believe, is the very sun that will rise tomorrow in the sky of your life.

* Keeping your focus is the game-plan for success.

* If good is your aim, where do you throw the ball.

* Opportunity and effort create an atmosphere for success.

* To measure your success, be sure not to use the ruler of another.

* Success may be measured, but joy has no limits.

* Success is the measure of man's efforts.

* Success is the result of timing and effort.

* Bravery is the expressed desire to succeed and to survive when all about you tells you that you cannot overcome.

* Success is contagious when you are in its presence.

*   Success is the reality of perseverance, acceptance, faithfulness, and the inspired will of God.

*   What we dream may become the success we come to know.

* To get a home-run, first you must hit the ball.

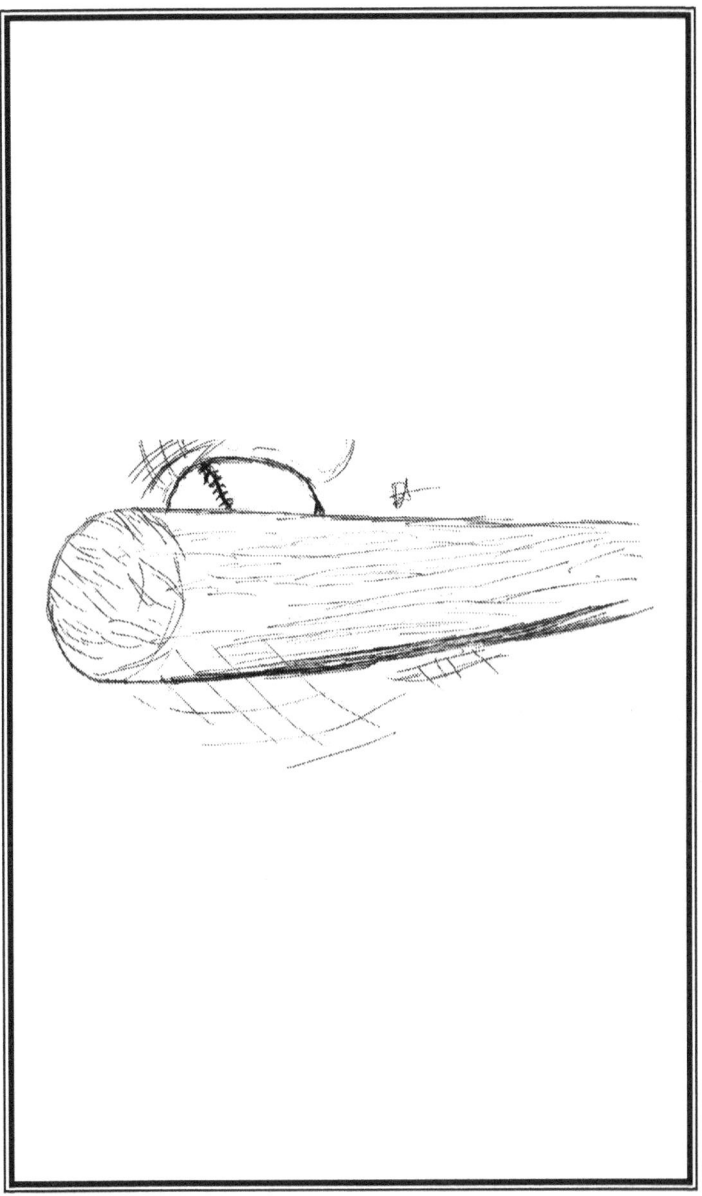

TODAY

* The life you lead is the result of the choices you have made and the ones you choose today.

* The significance of tomorrow is often sought in the silent meditation of today.

* A child's today may be the best of all eternity and the reward of precious moments you would have never known.

* Tomorrow we will view what together we shared today.

* Preparation of today is the "lighted path" of tomorrow.

* A grandmother is a soft touch of today and a sweet memory of tomorrow.

* The mishaps of yesterday may become the insights of today and the perhaps of tomorrow.

* What we share today will be what we remember tomorrow.

* The promise of today will find expression in the joy of tomorrow.

* Make today your best, it is the only TODAY you will have.

* Today can be the best; tomorrow can be the first; and yesterday can be remembered.

* What we prize today will be the memory of tomorrow.

* Tomorrow finds its way into today because its plan begins with the now.

* A grandson is the joy of today, the dreams of yesterday, and the legacy of tomorrow.

TRUTH

* Telling the truth is the only way to discover what a lie is.

* Truly no one ever knows the truth behind the smile except God.

* The hand of truth never points a finger.

* The tender heart tells the truth when the hardened heart tells a lie.

* Telling the truth brings dividends; lying cost more in interest than it is worth.

* Truth has no boundaries, and it ultimately is the winner in the game of life.

* When you listen with your soul, you will discover truth within the words.

* Truth has no need to be re-written.

UNDERSTANDING

* Knowledge is the core; understanding is the heart; and divinity is the answer.

* The way to a child's heart is through true understanding and love.

* Understanding comes when you seek the answer with an open mind.

* Generosity is the fruit which grows from the planting of the seed of understanding.

* Understanding is the hand that sprinkles kindness across a day.

* Understanding and compassion find expression when you invite them in.

* To truly understand how someone else feels tells you that you have been where they are right now.

* Generosity is born out of understanding the meaning of deprivation.

VISION

*   Vision is the expressed dream of the soul's search for goodness.

*   In order to arrive where you desire, first you must imagine where you are going and know where you have been.

*   Vision is the means by which you can see clearly without knowing where you are.

*   To have a vision means that you understand that tomorrow is dependent on that for which you aspire without any promise of it coming true.

*   What you can imagine can come true.

* If visions were dreams, how would you dream?

* Allow no one to dissuade you from your dreams; for your vision may be the precursor of your dreams.

* Vision of tomorrow is viewed in terms of today.

WISDOM

*   You cannot live in praise and condemnation at the same time.

*   Common sense is based on the failures of mankind.

*   If you are not happy, a spouse will not be enough to get you to that state.

*   When you see a silver lining in the sky of your life, be sure to remember that the silver lining is created when sunshine spreads across a cloudy life.

*   satan is a snake; and if he had no one to bother, he would bite his own tail and blame himself.

* When you hold the hand of joy, your path seems a little brighter.

* If you are true to your gift, it will be true to you.

* Condemn not what you know not.

* What you remember may be the most priceless treasure you possess.

* The morning dew is the anointing on a new day.

* Knowledge leads to maturity; maturity leads to wisdom; wisdom leads to kindness; kindness leads to understanding; and understanding leads to compassion.

* Time can be repeated and used well or disrespected and squandered.

* Knowledge comes with experience; wisdom comes with knowledge and understanding; knowledge, wisdom,

and understanding find expression in words.

* If sickness is a rainy day, then I wish for you sunshine on a soft summer morn.

* When you look into the heavens, remember that my thoughts of you far outnumber the stars.

* Protection hovers while innocence plays.

* Simple pleasures can make the most profound difference in your day when you allow them space.

* Nature sings a song of the heart and shares a melody of innocence.

* Perception is founded in a simple act.

* Sharing time with a brother makes for a great life.

* When children play, protection is divinely ordered.

* The innocence of children playing reveals divinity in its truest form.

* Fine men are like fine china; they are hard to find and hard to keep.

* A lazy day may be happiness at its best.

* Tiredness is sometimes the condition of a "willing spirit".

* No gift comes with a price-tag.

* Timing may be the fire beneath the pot.

* A gift is never competition to another gift for its value lies within itself.

* Detours are only road signs.

* Peace may be a simple walk in the sunshine and a breeze across your face.

* Laughter of the soul spreads as sunshine spreads across a day.

* A light never truly goes out; it just shines in a different galaxy.

* If wisdom could be bought, many millionaires would be very wise.

* Force does not create an atmosphere of tranquility.

* Water bathes the body as tears bathe the soul.

* The sparkle of the diamond reflects the light of the soul.

* When man realizes he is over the hill, he wonders where he got off the road.

* Where butterflies fly, happiness follows.

* Holiness abounds where welcomed.

* If you could buy a cup of joy, what would be the cost?

* Unnoticed moments in any given day may become the most significant times we ever know.

* Oh the joy of the search; for it is through seeking that we discover the true meaning of loss.

* When there is light, shadows fail to linger.

* You cannot cry and talk at the same time.

* The tapestry of marriage is the weaving of two souls.

* To be thankful, you first must be needful.

* Goodness seeks its own level.

* Joy is the expression of happiness without bounds.

* Illness is an equalizer of mankind.

* Time is negligible when eternity is the gage.

* Privacy allows for dignity in struggle.

* The sunshine of the soul lights the way for others to see.

* If you look toward tomorrow, you cannot see the yesterdays of your life.

* Every season holds a surprise of nature that inspires the soul.

* The only difference between red and black is the view.

* Money, age, and wisdom are not necessarily present simultaneously.

* Fleeting time sends a greeting to tomorrow.

* A sunny soul brings the dullest day alive.

* If you are not with me in the dingy, you cannot be with me on the ship.

*   Without divinity, prosperity has no meaning.

WORDS

* Words you say and deeds you do are like children you send out to play, but they always bring friends home with them.

* For every word, there is a ripple on the heart of man.

* Listen not to negativity; its language is impure.

* Last words sometimes fall on fertile hearts.

* After you think twice, it may be okay to speak once.

* Why say an unkind word that will one day at the time you need it the most come back to you in sentence form.

* What is spoken in unkindness results in pain.

* Any word spoken in kindness is never wasted.

* Never doubt that what you say or do is ever forgotten; for God has an eternal hard-drive.

* What the heart knows often cannot be expressed in words, but the heart knows how to smile.

* The tender heart is the custodian of soft words.

* What you say shows your true colors more than the colors in the rainbow of your life.

* When you start to speak, be sure your words are tempered by your heart.

* The tally of your words and deeds is kept beside the bed of God who never sleeps.

* Have you ever thought that the last good-bye and the first hello you will ever say will be eternal?

* Silence is sometimes the best manager of your soul.

* Words are the water that refreshes the souls of others.

* "No" may be the best "Yes" you ever heard.

* Silence allows the spirit within to speak.

* When you listen, you will discover that words, tones, and thoughts become the flowers of your day.

* There are times to speak, times to be silent, times to think, times to think

before you speak, and times to reflect upon all words you have spoken.

* Warm words melt a cold heart.

* Words tell the story of the heart's desires.

* The paper beneath the pen is the canvas for the painting of words.

* Fun and happiness often are found in the simple things we do and words we say.

* A silent tongue is a powerful tool.

* A mother listens to coos and words.

* Never waste a word because it may be the last word heard by man and the first word heard by God.

* Inferior is not a word God uses to describe His creation.

Summary

Throughout her book of aphorisms, Juanita Pittman-Brown has shared her southern culture and heritage. It is her hope that the truths which have evolved from her being a mother and the insight of what it is like growing up in the South have inspired you and brought you joy and enlightenment.

978-0-595-45774-8
0-595-45774-6